1440

POST & RAIL

OTHER BOOKS *by* ERICA FUNKHOUSER

Earthly
Pursuit
The Actual World
Sure Shot and Other Poems
Natural Affinities

POST & RAIL

poems | Erica Funkhouser

LOST HORSE PRESS
Sandpoint, Idaho

ACKNOWLEDGMENTS

I am grateful to the John Solomon Guggenheim Foundation for helping to provide the time in which this book was conceived and to Nicolas Brown for his eloquent conception of space-time.

Cover Art: Brian Sharp.
Author Photo: Nubar Alexanian.
Book & Cover Design: Christine Holbert.

FIRST EDITION

This and other LOST HORSE PRESS titles may be viewed online at www.losthorsepress.org.

LIBRARY OF CONGRESS CATALOGING-IN-PUBLICATION DATA
Cataloging-in-Publication Data may be obtained from the Library of Congress.
ISBN 978-0-9981963-8-1

A person is a line and an eye.

—*Simone Shen*

#1

The post is lowly. One may be a pillar of the community; who's a post?
With more elevation, it becomes a pole; with less, a stump. Some girth

is required. Plumpness of the sedentary. No figure to speak of. Minus
a few inches it's a stake. Column implies a surrounding edifice. None.

Humming with resin when fresh: confidence of the newly sunk. Come,
lend me your elbows. Soon it goes gray and softens, softens into time.

#2

Against the weight of a Black Angus steer, the repetitively delicate staves
of the fence rails quiver with cow sounds. No lowing, nothing comic-book,

not a moo from these glacial non-Daisys. A half ton of rump back and forth
against weathered pine; a shoulder reordering the universe. If boulders could

breathe, they'd make this music. Leaners, my father calls them. One piece
of fence goes, the whole thing collapses. Some days the cows go nowhere.

#3

Stepping off the school bus to the street, climbing the granite slabs to the path
to the kitchen door, we hear our mother: *Don't come home until you've found*

a cow. They escape complacently, wandering Monument Street as if they were
station wagons, or veering off into the woods, where they stop among dogtooth

violets to doze. We are the agitated ones, with our need to be elsewhere, free,
among friends. Our fists throb with plucked grass to tempt the bored foragers.

#4

If you wait long enough in front of the fence, hill and henhouse and sky
acquire the same restrained gray as the posts and rails, even if a whirling

sun on its way down sets aflame tractor, rooster and ragweed. The gray
comes round, comes round. The day is weathered. Those men listed on

ships' manifests as *labourers*, if listed at all—*James M, age 20, of Derry, of
Donegal, one sister*—their eyes turned from green to gray as they crossed.

#5

At the center of our galaxy, a black hole. We know this, despite its invisibility, because the black hole's fathomless gravity tugs at stars

as they whirl by. Inside, every invisible thing is compressed into a singularity. "The trouble with death," wrote Henry James, is that it

smooths the folds of those whom we love, reducing to one or two points the *swarm of possibilities.* I launch myself into the swarm.

#6

To Bernard and Sara the first child is born, 1875, Chest Springs. Charles Henry.
In two years, Mary Emma, in Liberty. Two years later, in Panic, Robert Shirley.

From pillar to post. Bernard down the mines. Sara barely 20. Reynoldsville in
1883, twins: Joseph Milo dead at 3, James Ira. Some time later, place unknown,

Mathias Ura. 1889, in Coalport, Fredric Bernard. Clyde Orin, 1891, in Frugality,
unincorporated home of Frugality Coal and Coke. Here only deaths are recorded.

#7

My mother never told us her father was a twin, the second boy buried
before he turned four. She never said the McFeeleys were Catholics.

She was anti-union despite the fact that her father, all his life a miner
for Berwind White Coal, was let go when emphysema disabled him.

Nor did she say that the store where she worked at the jewelry counter
was the company store, or that the Polish boy who walked into town to

flirt with her over chocolate sodas came from Scalp Level, a coal patch
for the workers at Eureka Mines 30 - 40. She did say she loved to play

tennis, loved to pick fruit at her mother's family farm, our grandmother
whose recipe for bread and butter pickles begins, *Pick 100 cucumbers.*

Her father was a *hard man,* she said, as if he'd made himself that way.
She was born tiny, graceful and tough. *Tough* she'd say, if we whined.

#8

How does anyone learn to see? Split rail fences proclaim here and there, us and them, and divide the world into three empires. Pasture and insect in the lowest.

The bodies of grazing animals in the second, their muzzles of leather and their muzzles of pink parfait offering up gobs of grassy slobber to apple-filled hands.

In the empire beyond touch, onyx of crows in high branches, everything hidden in green tunnels. With time, things give up and move, letting themselves be seen.

#9

What did they carry onto the brig Bartley, the brig Madawaska, bound for
St. John? The shirts on their backs, their turfy shoes, punk of the bog still

rich in their brimmed caps, a lack of alternatives, a mother's handkerchief.
Shoulders square, hands square, knees not yet blown. What small thing did

they keep folded in flannel in the square breast pocket of that knitted vest?
Stalk of flax? Carding of fog from the last soft hour of April? First kiss?

#10

They stretch. They grasp. They crack. They hover. They captivate. They cradle. They slip. They soften. They whistle you near, don't let you through.

Small things live on them. Spiders their color, beetles other colors. On them lichen establish colonies, rain gardens moss. To the ant a road, to the kingbird

an interlude. They join. They distinguish. Into the yonder. Under your nose. Rails in threes. As much the nothing between parts as the parts slid together.

#11

In every post, three long rough holes that could be the work of woodpeckers. The nearest neighbor, similarly buried and thrice shot through, stands six feet

distant—taciturn, upright Yankees. Daniel Webster buried his finest horses standing up, saddled and bridled, prepared to work when their master's bones

grew cold. The rails, tapered ends nestled in place, need not touch the earth. *Dreamers*, our mother laughs. We lie in the pasture, listening to the dreams.

#12

The last gasp in the life of a large star—a black hole. All along
its rim lie the points of no return we call the event horizon, the

boundary beyond which nothing, not even light, can escape the
black hole's gravitational pull. So much gravity that if our earth
were to fall into it, it would be compressed into a penny. In this
cosmic darkness, no one can see, even with devices, any of the

losses, if losses is the right word for the disappearance of matter
and light never seen by anyone. Here space is swallowing itself.

No wonder we love the little living stars from which we design
our constellations. They shimmer carelessly as we shape them

into the queen of Ethiopia or a bull, ancient stories sketched in
light. From here it's possible, is it not, to hear them listening?

#13

From Bonefoble and from Maldory they came, their parishes old names
for nightmares, their empty stomachs unaccounted for in any tally book.

If there was flaxseed to plant, they worked, the labors of linen handily
doing in whole families. In Pennsylvania they sowed flax once more,

counted now as *Labourers.* The cloth in which Egyptian royalty were
wrapped, the sturdy stuff of Roman sails. Old world work or new, each

step bends the back: stems scrupulously weeded to grow upright must
be gently eased from their rooty grip. Bundled sheaves are piled into

stooks to dry, then steeped in pondwater. Retting is rotting, and the air
fills with the funk of monsters. After a second drying comes scutching,

the hammering of woody stems to separate the soft blond fibers before
they're heckled, or straightened out with ever finer combs. Once spun,

the yarn is boiled and dried. Once woven, the cloth is whitened for
shirts and dresses and beetled to bring coarse threads closer together.

Now one may scissor out the shape of one's beloved above the waist
or swaddle a mewling newborn. This was the work of the first days,

before the men went down to pick the precious crop lying acres below
daylight—the ferns once blithely free now compacted into filthy coal.

#14

We slide the rails in and out of their holes to make fences for the horses
to jump. We tie hair ribbons onto the rails to feel more equestrian, even

if the horses are old and we're riding bareback, without bridles. Bravely
at a trot we clear the lowest rung, triumphant. We've guided an animal

many times our own weight over an obstacle of our own making. Last
thing over is the elated tail—a whole different creature, groomed to fly.

#15

One night he stepped out of the mantrap portal, wiped his hands on the tail of a comet, then waded in Paint Creek till the water had run over his boots and

the fish had licked his toes clean. When he got home, before he opened the door, he took off his head and shook the coal dust onto the street. When his wife gave

him bread and tea, he gave her salmon with lemons. They kissed before the fire. When his children showed him their red feet, he cobbled shoes from butterscotch.

#16

The forest is where we go to be alone and not alone. Trails ample and
narrow—for carts, for wanderers, for hunters, for the hunted. We can

choose to travel as if we were delivering milk to a neighbor a hundred
years ago, or in the delicate first steps of a fawn. The porcupine sleeps

on a branch. Between trees, the sudden trajectory of a blue jay or the
silent articulation of an owl. Of course the creatures who live hidden

in the forest slide behind a stump if they're shy, blink yellow eyes if not. Wherever there is a rootcellar, someone is still in residence. In

the pond lives a thing that shows only its crenellated tail. When we enter the forest to look for cows, we hope we won't find one. They

squeeze their huge square bodies between trees, like glacial erratics. Not mean. Stubborn. And the only way to move a cow is sideways.

#17

On the day it is announced that gravitational waves have been heard,
as these things are heard, by a wobble of needles, I read that a sense

of place is *the torque between temperament and terrain.* A personal chirp in
one's universe. It helps me to understand my mother if I think of her

as an event that took place in distant space and, because its waves
could travel unimpeded by matter, has finally brought its birdsong

to earth. Over a billion years ago two black holes collided; now our instruments of detection have become so elegant and so acute in their

L-shaped tunnels in Louisiana and Washington and in the laboratories of listening, that we can eavesdrop on creation. One day I'll hear the

answer to my mother's *Who do you think you are?* She loved to sit in big man-made spaces—gymnasiums, opera houses—difficult to spot.

#18

When she wasn't speaking, we heard the phoebe splash, one season
turn its back upon the next, the pink lady slippers slip into extinction.

She didn't point or name; she might have blinked or waved her hand.
She liked to move, she couldn't keep from moving; silence was a way

of being still. The stillness lay inside her like an anvil. We could hear
the words being hammered into sparks and her relief as they died out.

#19

On the immobile rails even the insects have fallen asleep, or they're
at home in their colonies, the weavings and scrapings and tunnelings

where they produce more of themselves in the dark. Summer noon.
Between the rails, the afternoon trembles, a mirage of promises and

promises delivered. Cavalcade of white steeds, plumed riders. Wild
singletons all, none complicit in the day in day out fretwork of family.

#20

In Thomas Mann's *The Magic Mountain,* a former guest at the TB sanatorium refers to residents condemned to rest cures on deck chairs as *The Horizontals.*

Like patients *etherized upon a table,* but not. On their south-facing balconies they inhale rejuvenating alpine air while wrapped in camelhair and dreaming

of *blanquette de veau* and the pale young Russian wraith in furs who arrived after dinner. Finally they've escaped *the yellow smoke that slides along the street.*

They do not fret about a marriage, as Prufrock does. Any passion they incite or seize comes with a guarantee of brevity. No one leaves cured, and besides,

World War is on its way to make young men forever horizontal. The clinic's clean lines, deep verandas and wide sunny windows, along with the invention

of poured concrete, will give us modern architecture. If there are *Verticals* in Mann's novel, they are a waterfall, a column of mercury and a coffee pot.

#21

Vertical questions emanate from the posts in front of me and the posts all the way down to the lower pasture, the kinds of questions posed by something buried up

to its ankles and kept in place as much by the rails driven through its three orifices as by its own footing. Really it is all one question: How are you connected to the

grass beneath your feet, the air circling your elbows, the clouds circumnavigating your thoughts? With the shift of one letter bright as a new nail, post becomes poet.

#22

fence post gate post lamp post mile post goal post sign post corner post
outpost hitching post listening post starting post bed post trading post

postcard postmark postman postwoman postpone postscript postilion
postmeridian postprandial posthumous post mortem post bellum post

hoc post-Classical post-industrial post-colonial post-apocalyptic post-
haste post-nasal post-traumatic post-rational post-partum post-modern

#23

Coming from weathered tongues, the low voices of the soft rails
grow ever softer, ever more susceptible. The posts fare no better,

perpetual aloftness requiring them to swallow rainstorms whole.
They splinter, they sponge, they disintegrate. It's only a matter

of time before we see ourselves every place we look, incapable
of negative capability. This day the fence is full of self-regard.

#24

If you read between the rails you'll see a pair of coffins carrying empty space, then you'll see the spaces emptying like cornucopias their harvest of history:

coffin ships coffin boxcars coffin borders coffin laws coffin wars coffin offices coffin officers coffin corners coffin classrooms coffin cupboards coffin options.

Maybe you'll read the rails and hang on their limned assertions: we got from there to here, a narrow escape. We keep to ourselves. An improvised survival.

#25

More real than his six children, than his wife, with her deep-bodied
love of hounds and flowery scraps that may be pieced into coverlets,

her way of sniffing fresh biscuits and declaring them pure gold—
more real than this the other world he visits in dream, where trees

open to let a hunted man enter, the thistle softens to a pillow to hum
a wanderer to sleep, and any bird will tell you the next day's weather.

#26

Evening will always be horizontal, will always be a gray rail sliding
into darkness, a gray mare lying down in her stall or a gray-breasted

bird aligning itself with a branch. Earth receiving the sun. A well-
used body resting its whole length against another well-used body

with a pleasure surpassing that of dawn. The trough of exhaustion
allows them to seal their eyes and go slack, to lie as one in the dark.

#27

At daybreak, if they're awake, his children swerve to escape his glance.
He tries not to touch them before he goes down for fear their warm hair

will be the last soft thing in his hands. He makes himself into a newt to
work all day; still, at supper, the children see a stooped giant. Like the

ferns turned to coal by the pressure of centuries, his own words bear no
resemblance to their original frivolity. Once he must have played with

sound as a fern plays with light, creating color on a gray day, shadows when the day is bright. A fountain of words, he must once have been.

Aren't we all? He can remember singing to an oak tree, resting his lips against the rough bark to make his music heard. His fingers remember

the powdery curiosity of each of his six babies as they squirmed in his arms, their eager babble. He fears his silence is a coward's resignation

#28

My mother got up earlier than the rest of us. Summer and winter, always the first in the kitchen. I think she loved us most when she

was making our breakfast, while we were still asleep upstairs and no one was bossy or bratty or sulking or holding two chubby arms

out and asking to be picked up. Before that, there were just muffins rising in the oven, oatmeal expertly bubbling, seven empty glasses.

#29

Words. Minutes. Answers. A lap. A laugh. A kiss. To be made much
of. To be remarkable. To be remarked upon. These are some of what

we wanted, we noisy chicks. But she did not like words, did not trust or
enjoy them. If they had a purpose, fine, but otherwise they were suspect.

A lover of opera, she never listened to the ones in English. If she listened
to us, it was one at a time. We'd find her icing a cake or selecting thread

for her endless mending, and we'd hold onto her tweed skirt and set forth on our tale of triumph or of woe. She might look up from her work to say

That's something, which meant nothing, but if she said it with a smile, we kept talking. Her smile was crooked; she could look annoyed at the same

time she looked happy. She never added to our stories, and she knew the minute we started telling lies. *That's enough* she'd say, restoring silence.

#30

Is it silence that hones the edge of time or the solid sentences
that will not alter even when the void between them bends and

shakes? Is the edge impediment or gift or error? We live on
the borderland between reality and dream, believing in both.

Now into our revery struts a Rhode Island Red, or to the task
at hand falls the intangible handle of someone else's memory.

#31

To slide into the seam the men make a thread of their bodies, lying
on one side or on their backs to face the face of coal. There's room

to grunt, to spit, to wedge an ax. Room for a low basket. Not room
to kneel or stoop or scratch, to flick a drop of water off. The nicker

of a mule might reach them, or the breathing of the earth as it shifts
around their bodies. Each slender breath a reassessment of the risk.

#32

He never dreamed of flying—a good dream let him swim parallel
to shore, a glossy seal surfacing at his side and staying there, only

whiskers away and breathing effortlessly—but he did dream in his
waking hours of buying a silver Airstream like the one he'd seen

in Pittsburgh, its aerodynamic chrome a cross between a breadbox
and a DC-17, its front end riveted as nobly as the helmet of a god.

In 1949, he and Lizzie bought an Airstream Clipper and moved to southern California. In one of the few photographs ever taken of

James Ira McFeeley, he is dying of black lung while balancing in his generous palms two grapefruits plucked from a roadside grove.

The sun's diameter is a hundred times larger than the earth's, and those orbiting grapefruits are a hundred times larger than the sun.

#33

Filthy valuable, the coal. Edward Berwind, son of a German guitar-maker,
appointed to the Naval Academy by President Lincoln, became the *macher*

of coal. Filthy with *new money*, he was snubbed on Fifth Avenue when he
completed his mansion there. By 1896 he was the largest individual holder

of bituminous coal in the country, perhaps the world. Railroads, the Navy,
steamships out of Philly and New York, soon the N.Y. subways: all running

on Berwind's coal. By 1901 he'd built *The Elms* in Newport. No children,
but at the house-warming imported monkeys played in the palms. Famous

for refusing to bargain, his mines were the coal fields' last open shops. In
Windber, PA, his name inverted, and in Berwind, WV, his name left right,

he lived by one rule: Own your miners. When the miners finally went on
strike, they were given five days to vacate their company houses. In tents

they lived, in chicken coops and cow sheds, in underbrush, *the womenfolk old and hollow-eyed before their time, the children undersized.* December 1922

came with a vengeance. Berwind and J. P. Morgan, historic union of two, landed in our colorful social studies books, *Titans in the golden age of coal.*

Geniuses of consolidation and expansion. When Newport society ignored Berwind, he had his signature moustache carved on every flower urn that faced Bellevue Avenue. *Strike to End Fear* the union pamphlets said, *Fear of The Boss, The Spotters, The Coal and Iron Police.* After sixteen bitter months,

when John L. Lewis negotiated a national settlement for the UMWA, over 70,000 non-union miners nation-wide were left out. The Berwind men had

to wait another decade in the towns where their employer owned *absolutely the banks, the theatre, a number of public halls, the town newspaper,* and all the *public*

service plants, the public officials—the burgess, squires, councilmen and the police.
Also the store in Windber where my mother later sold birthstone rings

and necklaces of artificial pearl. I can see her in a cloche, at 18, when her
father and the others got their union; I can't see her in 1922, when she was

8 years old. Where'd she live? She never spoke of this except to dismiss
John L. Lewis with the poisonous hiss she reserved for spoken eloquence.

#34

Others have ancestors who still speak to them, are speaking to them right now, enlarging the moment. They have been summoned by ceremony, by reverence.

Like all of us these ancient people have a fragrance they prefer, a corner of the world, a time of day. Or they come by surprise; they'd been watching and saw

now was the time to appear. Who is watching me? Who speaks? A presence in the fence posts, in the rails. Something with no eyes, no mouth and not what we'd call a body, but watching, offering, nudging. Compared to the work they do, my own work is useless. They encourage me. Uselessness is a luxury they

believe in. I can tell from the great distances between each of their words that they are in no hurry. They once made their own long and difficult crossings

in order to reach a new world. If I journey far to reach one word, they will be patient. A ridge of bark, the canted antenna of a moth: it could be anywhere.

#35

A small chirp lets us in on one of the darkest, most energetic events in
the universe: one black hole colliding with another a billion years ago,

unheard until we found a way to listen to the universe. My mother's
silence took a long time to reach me, daughter-time being governed by

its own invisible physics. Her silence was not an absence of sentiment,
nor was it chosen—we could see feeling sprinting through her body,

and we could see her chafe against it when she wanted us to know one thing we absolutely had to do. It's not that she didn't listen to us—she

did—but we knew that if we talked too much she'd think of something we had to do. And it wasn't an affliction; she looked happy when she

sat alone at the kitchen table, smoking a cigarette, the inhalation at the corner of her bright red lips and the papery tapping of the ash against a thin white saucer the only sound for miles. If she'd been writing a letter, the silence would have been a way to wait for words, but she didn't even

send a postcard when she was away. Someone else's silence might have made room for instruction, memory or God, but hers wasn't professional

or devotional. It comes to me—not the explanation, but another way of hearing what she'd never have put into words: her silence was a way of emptying her body of everything that interfered with movement. She was always in motion; it was this restless energy that spoke for her. Watching

her slip into her boots, we knew we'd soon be in the woods; glimpsing her smile as we resurfaced from the pond, we knew our diving was improving;

putting our hands out to take a plate of food and feeling her hands on the other side, firm, not giving up our supper until she was convinced it was good, we knew everything,—almost everything—we would need to know. Vanishingly small, these ripples in the fabric of space-time, generated by

cataclysms in the early universe, yet here they are, a lost world coming back to us chirp by chirp, if we will just keep listening to the new carrier

of information, the gravitational field. My mother had a way of alerting us to the fact that we were loved; we had to supply the words ourselves.

#36

After the thick soft ears pointing east and west, the first thing you notice about Black Angus cows is the wide forehead. They hold it in front of you, as dark

and shiny as a cast iron wood stove. Their eyes lack mobility, so they move the whole stove up and down, left and right, slowly taking you in. We spend hours

looking into those quiet eyes and we notice nothing, but when we rest our heads against the galaxies of coal-black fur, warmth pours into us from another world.

#37

A working definition of vertical. Eye-alignment suffices. My father's plumb bob
remains in the toolshed. Horizontal means simply a line in line with the horizon,

barely visible from here. Boulders and streams require improvisation and mild
swearing. The post-hole digger has long handles that end in scratched red half-

cylinders of steel, a giant version of the silvery tongs my mother uses to arrange
spaghetti on our plates. She does not whistle as she works, but my father does.

#38

The same thing over and over again, but the opposite of boredom: the post
and rail fences surround the corral, the pastures and, with a fine mesh wire

tacked to them, the henhouse, the puppy pen, the duck pond. Attempts to
keep the foxes out, the snakes. A roof of chicken wire against the hawks.

Each gate has its heavy iron loop of a latch, or its oiled bolt or its frayed
lariat of baling twine. Opening a gate, turning a page: it is all the same.

#39

Beyond post and rail the orchard roars, the pyramid of gold and black
manure manufactures earthworms, the stream gobbles the grassy bank

down to root and bedrock, the woodpile sparks with mice and snakes
and fire ants. Foxes part the tall grass. Dogs rustle rabbits back into

their holes. Among the buds of one apple tree, honeybees swarm like
an animated burlap sack, frantic to discover where they will go next.

#40

One day the world becomes uninhabited color. A field of blue above
a field of green. Two posts and three rails the gray of dried rain hold

it all in place. The blue adamant, the green ambivalent. Or the green
a spiral galaxy, the blue non-operational. A blue entrance put off by

green tension. A turbulent reversal where either color meets a slash
of gray, whose small blows kindle worlds safe from the eye of time.

#41

For the indignity of being twigless limb, cramped bannister, brittle as only the severed and split are brittle, it is necessary to praise the rail.

For the post that does nothing but open its heart in three places and hold still, more praise is required. Exposed as they are, their effort

one we are so accustomed to that we no longer see it, they impel us to be still before them, to discover where in our selves we are them.

#42

The weather in his dreams was always mild, so when he woke up
in California, he knew he was dreaming. Wide rows of citrus trees

called to him, and when he started walking, the path didn't narrow.
So much blue sky that he could close his eyes without fearing the

day was lost. And the sun. How could a thing so kind not grow
tired of giving its kindness away? He and Lizzie got a Dalmation

and the dog ran so fast between the grapefruit trees that its spotted body turned into an arrow of gray. In a real dream, he rode on the

dog's back in the shape of a feather, also gray, and like a sailboat seized by the wind, they flew toward the horizon. When they got

there, the horizon was as real as the rim of a cup, and into it they dived, dog and feather, and already that must have been ages ago.

NOTES

#5 Henry James, from "James Russell Lowell," *Atlantic Monthly*, January 1892

#17 Frances McCue, from the Introduction to *The Car That Brought You Here Still Runs* (Seattle: University of Washington Press, 2010)

#20 Thomas Mann, *The Magic Mountain*, translated by John E. Woods (New York: Vintage International, a division of Random House, Inc., 1996) and T.S. Eliot from *The Love Song of J. Alfred Prufrock*

#30 David Hirshfield, *Report from the NYC Commission on Labor Conditions at the Berwind White Coal Mines in Somerset and Other Counties*, appointed by John F. Hylan, Mayor of NYC, December 1922